A Cézanne Haibun

Maitreyabandhu

Published 2019 by
Smith|Doorstop Books
The Poetry Business
Campo House
54 Campo Lane
Sheffield S1 2EG

ISBN 978-1-912196-24-1

Designed and Typeset by Utter
Printed by Biddles Books

Smith|Doorstop Books are a member of Inpress:
www.inpressbooks.co.uk. Distributed by NBN International,
Airport Business Centre, 10 Thornbury Road, Plymouth PL6 7PP

The Poetry Business gratefully acknowledges the support
of Arts Council England.

Supported by
ARTS COUNCIL
ENGLAND

'Almendra', Sierra Aitana

As was instructed, I lifted up my eyes
to shadowed gorse and patchy-shadowed pine,
wild grasses, flowers without a Latin name,
that I might purify myself again.

That horse chestnut, the heart's meandering,
the rancid mess of it while songbirds sing
a song that I have talked about too much,
as if I really cared for them enough.

I'd hoped the dappled gorse and thistle flower
might be enough to fill the limping hour
with limpid thought or with a crystal heart,
instead of being where all the ladders start.

Every day now I go down to the ruined cottage to take in the view – spear grass (well, that's what I'm calling it), flax, a great coppery thistle losing its head to every breeze that comes along. The month stretches ahead like an idling train, each day an empty carriage. One tap. No electricity. A few dark pans. The phone wrapped up in a sock. Re-reading Cézanne's letters – impatience with paint suppliers, complaints about the weather, confiding in Louis Aurenche 'Sometimes I have flights of enthusiasm, more often painful disappointments' – it's the lateness that hurts, the lateness and the loneliness. London under cloud. Alicante in fine weather. A wheelie bag under the bed.

.

The coffeepot reminds
me of the coffeepot
in *Woman with a Coffeepot*,

his portrait of a teaspoon,
a teacup and (probably)
Madame Brémond.

After a measly thunderstorm that I'd hoped would get louder but didn't, a warbler settled on a thorn. I sauntered back to the hut. Two long-tailed tits fluttered in front of me, stopped, then flew away again like pageboys in a fairytale. Cézanne was always thinking he should be somewhere else. When in Paris, grumbling over the Zola portrait, he'd want to be back in Aix – missing trains, making to-do lists, crossing things out, complaining to Pissarro about his 'excruciatingly annoying' family. Writing to his boyhood friend, the cabinetmaker and joiner Justin Gabet, he concludes '*Bon courage!* And don't forget the extinguisher of streetlights.'

Every year I come back
  to this minor dwelling,
a limestone trough the moon
  looks into, and think of him,

perpetually old in my mind,
  with easel and differently
sized brushes, curses
  and charm, gesticulations,

          talk that made the dishes rattle,
              old-style courtesies to maids
          and mademoiselles, and
              work of course, only work.

A grasshopper has turned up at the centre of the drystone arch that frames
the pine trees outside my hut: 'The venerable statesman who presides over
the political destinies of France has come to honour us with a visit.' Sending
awful poems to Zola, thanking him for the cigars that tasted of barley sugar
and caramel, Cézanne imagined the cigar smoke was Justine laughing at him:
'I touched her dress'. Meyer Schapiro finds evidence in one of the poems
for the young Cézanne's anxieties about his father. This leads Schapiro to
ask whether the painter's lifelong preoccupation with still life was in fact an
unconscious impulse to restore harmony to the family mealtime. Monsieur
Cézanne leans across the table, 'I'll be waiting to thump the first man who
comes within reach of my fist!'

              I chop logs
              and gather kindling

while Cézanne,
supervising
the construction
at Les Lauves,

deletes the balcony
and fancy tiling.

I have left a list of provisions (teabags, candles, soap) in a black dustbin next
to the track that runs winding through the valley. So it must be a Tuesday.
My toilet is a box about the size of a packing crate (it may in fact *be* a packing
crate). I have to step up to it and am indeed enthroned, surrounded by tall
pines, such grave courtiers. In a letter to Vollard, Cézanne writes 'I work
tenaciously ... I have made some progress. Why so late and with so much
difficulty?' And that about sums it up. I walk to the ruined cottage for the
sunset across the view. My mother, shooing us out of the Austin Princess,
insisted we watch the sunset at Devil's Mouth while my father searched for
copper wire and my brothers ran off. We got cold waiting, my sister, my
mother and I, catching the final rays. That must have been about the time I
was doing so badly at school my mother had to say 'CSE's aren't worth the

paper they're written on!' So let's hear it for late starters and slow learners. Let's hear it for those who struggle and don't know why they struggle but keep on struggling. Let's hear it for them – making a little progress after all.

> I sit all morning
>   without my glasses,
> unaccustomed to silence.

'The sun is so fierce the objects seem silhouetted, not only in black and white but in blue, red, brown and violet.' (Cézanne to Pissarro – L'Estaque, 2nd July 1876.) Today the light is petulant. When the sun comes out it's like my mother ironing, pressing down on brothers' shirts and socks. Then the heat goes out of everything because of a cloud. The pine trees alternate between vying for my attention and blending into a mess of colours smudged together on a palette. The wind is up, or several winds, testing individual treetops, branches, bunches of pine needles, giving each a little shake or even quite a big one. And I can't help thinking that I'm the centring eye, the god of my occasion. No birds to speak of – just a chough cussing its single syllable. The occasional wasp. The up and down of midges.

White roads. Low-lying pastures.
Grubbing for water-plants
or watching for eels.

A few stunted olive trees –
daytime lulled to evening
by some dreadful troopers' song.

The loneliness comes on around four o'clock with the first fading of the light. I break off three squares of chocolate and wait for the moon. There are no light effects, as such, in Cézanne. No gathering gloom; no darkness twittering between the trees. A Cézanne landscape is daylight-diffused-by-cloud (so he could better judge the forms). *The valley is going to sleep with a silvery beauty, a few vestigial colours left burning a little while longer, the heat going out of everything like chimneys.* But there are no women with their arms crossed. No theatres. No dances at the Moulin de la Galette. And now I come to think about it, no birds – no sparrows busy in the briar, no Mr and Mrs Magpie. Nothing, in other words, that couldn't be kept still. Oh, maybe there's a woman carrying a basket, down there in the Arc valley walking along a dust road with the mountain looming. But that brushmark may not be a person at all.

Above the Dragon's Back
an airbus
points my passage home.

I dreamt about Gary again last night, his full weight against me, kissing me
as if we were still in our first passion. Even when I woke it was as though
he was still there, turned away and facing the wall. After breakfast I walked
up to the bin for a shopping bag of vegetables and Tetra packs. The view
to a distant pockmarked ridge and an undecided sky makes me wonder
how Cézanne would have dealt with it – branches with a few pine needles
closing off the top, pine trunks pillaring the sides. Bending over stones
in the foreground, scimitar-like iris leaves – no flowers, a small green hell
– flourish in the welcoming heat. Van Gogh painted them in Arles. And
here he is with trembling hands in the back of Tanguy's shop showing the
painting to Cézanne. And here's Cézanne saying 'So you really are insane!'

What can I wish you
  but what you'd wish
yourself:

good studies
  in nature's presence,
a little confidence,

and work –
  Sic itur ad astra –
and then you'll reach the stars.

The days roll on, each pretty much the same. My daily chocolate ration. Pine trees and limestone. The ruined cottage with its dirty shuttered eyes. Ruskin wrote rapturously about rocks, drawing and painting them, studying them, seeing the mountain in them. O bread of earth! O church our congregation scatters over! There's a watercolour in Princeton, *Pine Trees and Rocks above the Château Noir,* that reminds me of Ruskin – sun-warmed stone, graphite-scribbles among the shadows. Cézanne might have painted it then turned to the lane winding up through the National Gallery past Van Gogh's summery wheatfield and Seurat's listless boys. The rocks tell you everything you need to know about the articulation of light and how each angled facet is a piano chord struck against the darkness of the world.

The gecko on the wall
is as still as Cézanne
would expect you to be –
Joachim Gasquet,
Ambroise Vollard,
Louis Guillaume –
if he painted you.

I was thinking about the first time a picture of mine became a painting (no, the second; the first was a portrait of my father from a photo of him standing by the stove). I'd been drawing in Myatt's Fields, listening to *Tristan und Isolde* on my Walkman. I couldn't distinguish the voices back then so it sounded like a woman screaming followed by a yelling man. Anyway, I was taken up in it, more or less, and the drawings I made seemed worth the *Liebestod*. Till then I'd wanted to say something about patriarchy and The Print Workers, but now I pitched in and painted. The picture became a jumbled box of colour. So one afternoon (it was nearly home time and, to put it rather grandly, I was in love at the time though it took me years to say so) I over-painted the sky, removing half the foliage at a lick. Suddenly, it was palpable I remember, suddenly the painting stepped forward like someone giving you their full attention. Except there was something wrong with the bottom left-hand corner, that bush there. So I moved it, ever so slightly. Angled it. The whole painting clicked into place as if one good shove was all it needed.

> The first bat
>   sewing
> the evening together
>
> with a cotton thread –
>   jammy dodger,
>   *Messerschmitt!*

'Would you be kind enough to give me his address and a word of recommendation?' wrote the advocate and art critic, Théodore Duret. He was trying to help. So what was Zola up to fobbing him off with 'I cannot give you the address of the painter that you seek. He is very much withdrawn'? Cézanne was writing to Madame Zola thanking her for her gift of paint-rags, 'I have several studies on the go, on grey and sunny days'.

An argument was brewing between *L'histoire naturelle et sociale d'une famille* and seven apples. Only in painting could Cézanne be entirely private and manifestly public at the same time – each stroke a movement of the mind moving into and beyond itself, each mark a whisper and a shout. Three years later Duret tried again, this time in a letter to Pissarro. 'In painting' he wrote 'I'm looking more than ever for that fabulous beast of the imagination, the five-legged sheep.'

Château Noir
built by a ruined coal merchant.

Bibémus spat upon
and blooded by Gaius Marius' troops.

The Great Pine
treated as portraiture.

What was it Bashō said (I think it was Bashō), 'What am I doing here? Why don't I just go home?' Boredom and loneliness. There's the chough's call.

And there's the wind, the old wind, sifting somewhere. I'd been thinking about my nephew's wedding, my eldest brother's eldest son. The wedding breakfast was held in a white marquee on my brother's land. My nephew was marrying a doctor's daughter and my mother, wearing a fascinator gripped in her thin white hair (she always hated hats or shopping for a dress), my mother said 'They're ever so easy to talk to, not at all hoity-toity.' I said 'No one says hoity-toity any more.' She replied 'Thirty years ago they wouldn't have given us the time of day.' I remember on the way back to London after the band arrived (it was chilly for a May evening), I remember reading on the train and Gary being cold. I glanced out of the window and a tube train came up alongside us, familiar yet unaccustomed, like the first time I saw my brother without his glasses. A row of moving windows moving with our moving and lit up, I suppose, like stories – someone yawning, a woman gazing at her phone, a couple with the man seeming to explain something, and an elderly woman with a Sainsbury's bag who might have been my mother feeling looked down upon and thinking 'Who are they to look down on us?' Then it was gone.

After the storm,
I heard

what I'd take to be   '
   plovers

if I was living by the sea –
   a lovely,
throaty call, winnowing
   and far off.

On days like this the light is biblical. The pines stand like Ahab and Hezekiah, the stones might be the stones of Judea, and look, there's the Burning Bush with Abraham threatening his son. Danchev is probably right, *L'Œuvre* didn't cause the rupture after thirty years of friendship 'with a feeling of time passing'. The friendship merely frayed, as friendships might, in misunderstandings and regret: Cézanne's tetchiness, Zola's ostentation and awful wife. They'd grown apart, each in his privacy thinking the other had lost touch, betrayed some cause they'd set out on in a boyhood of truancy and bathing. So often in the late letters Cézanne complains about the weather, starting work at four-thirty because it is too hot by eight and addles his brain. 'Everything you say in your letter is true. I'm plodding along in the same old way. Hello to maman and everyone who still remembers me.

Do you know where the little sketch of bathers is?' I go inside and make tea. The sun, meek today and mild, must be Jesus, wearing white raiment.

> No one knows what to do with us,
> even the gods have given up –
> a flutter in the juniper, a tipsy tail,
> an echo as the valley falls asleep.

A lizard crawls onto the woodblock where I have left my notebook and pen. On gravelly ground behind it, a platoon of ants, blackberry and twinkling, manhandle a broken snail shell, seeming to worry it from all angles. I don't reach for the notebook until the lizard climbs down, which it does in its own time, only scaring when I lift my hand. John Rewald, Cézanne's first biographer, didn't take to Madame Cézanne. He was looking for a god and no one can be a god in their own family. Cézanne's sisters, Marie and Rose, suspected Hortense of gold digging. Cézanne wrote 'My wife likes only lemonade and Switzerland' but in the late letters to his son he remembers her with affection and respect: 'I embrace you and maman with all my heart', 'a hug for you and maman', that sort of thing. To be a mother, as far as

Cézanne was concerned, was to be nonpareil, which makes me wonder if he was like my dad who always said, if my mother refused cocoa or an orange, 'Your mother is having an attack of the no-thank-yous' – that companionable love.

Supper out of the paella pan –
   olive oily, garlicky,
onions you could

eat like apples. The pan might be
   an *objet trouvé* in
a Picasso sculpture:

El Toreador Negro
   (with jug ears).
The last scrapings are best.

Rilke in the Elegies said the trees around a shrine *become* the shrine: old pilgrims standing around in all weathers with rough clothes and dirty feet.

I can hear the wind but the pine tree by my hut is breathless till someone seems to brush against it gently, setting everything a-shimmer: *The whole earth is full of his glory* (Isaiah 6:1-9). There's a watercolour in the V&A, not so big, with pinholes in the corners where he pinned it to the board. Just pencil lines and tentative patches of colour. The abutting and overlapping marks resist depiction. Mostly they locate us in our glimmery étude with such thoughtfulness – the pine trunks dancer-like and receding – that a walk in the wood gives us every reason to exist.

That must be him
walking back to the studio
because the weather

is too changeable – shifting
brilliances and fades –
to paint *sur le motif.*

After a long rain – not the inundation that turns the shaley paths into rivulets and carries the needles down but a slow persistent half-rain – the sky was grey enough to study without the perplexity of too much light and shade. I have started counting the days. I remind myself of an old man I nursed in the Coventry and Warwick. He was having an allergic reaction, to amoxicillin I think. He'd sit and shout out the days of the week – *Monday! Tuesday! Wednesday!* – in a declamatory crescendo. I don't know what reminded me of the story of Cézanne painting Mont Sainte-Victoire and some chump coming up behind – knife creases, a girlish voice. The man started lecturing Cézanne on Corot: 'These muted browns that teeter into green prove Corot to be our only teacher before nature.' That sort of thing. 'But this parti-coloured cavalcade, this blue burlesque … ' And so forth. Cézanne listened with his hands clasped together, head bowed. Screwing up his eyes in concentration, he let out a long, slow, rasping fart. 'That's better' he said.

The whole valley
seems deserted –
only clouds live here.

'Take this old body and hide it in the mountains.' That's how the Bashō poem ends. Amen to that. When I drop off my list of provisions at the bin

I have to leave a sign: a long stick with its end painted. And that's about all I have to do today – a middle-aged man from a seven-pub two-church one-newsagent stop-off on the way to Birmingham. The rocks couldn't care less. As he got older and more crotchety, Cézanne thought people were trying to get their hands on his money, which was why he ended up walking those five miles to the mountain despite his age and health, his bad foot, the knapsack of watercolours, the easel and the heat. Literally, given what happened, walking to his death. Emery had raised the price of the carriage to three francs return when Cézanne used to go all the way to the Château Noir for five.

Flies at their obsessive
  hand-washing,
ants among the provisions
  (UHT milk and sliced bread)

and every night
  under the kerosene lamp,
you, ageing decade
  by furious decade.

The light is fading and soon the pine trees will become a net to catch the silver fish. My mind is turning to home and to the things of home – sex and cinema. A hot shower. A flushing loo. I've got the floor to mop, the rug to thrash, the usual dishes to wash and put away. 'The love of physical and moral ugliness is a passion like any other' wrote Rochefort in *L'Intransigeant* addressing Zola and his 'ordinary painters'. It made Cézanne's hands shake when he opened the Paris papers. Once, when they both happened to be in Aix at the same time, someone asked if the author of *Les Rougon-Macquart* intended to visit his old friend. 'What's the point of seeing that failure again?' Zola replied. But when news of Zola's death reached him, sixteen years after the publication of *L'Œuvre*, Cézanne locked himself inside the studio and wept. No one dared go in.

Sugar bowl. Three pears.
Blue cup. (The painting
that appears in the
upper right-hand corner
of *The Artist's Father
Reading a Newspaper*.)
Signing himself up.

'I am waiting till four when the carriage will come and take me to the river. It's cooler there. I felt very well there yesterday.' I decide to go to the ruined cottage for one last look. The road, more of a track than a road, leads to the road that leads to the town that leads to the airport. Calvin Klein and Burberry. My nephew's wedding reminded me of the time when he was five or six. He had come to London with the family, and looking at the reproduction hanging in our kitchen, a still life from the Musée d'Orsay, exclaimed 'That's a Cézanne!' and everyone was amazed.

> Rain-parched colours,
>   flint track and
> pine bark
>
> blur into patches
>   that – is it a nuthatch? –
> chirrups through.

Waking up to the usual sore belly and stiff neck, I mull over my failure and the failure of mulling over my failure, the vanity of it, et cetera. Then

I'm like a young bachelor, leaving the washing up in the sink. The sun is out, florid and stroppy as usual, not a hint of breeze. 'The only thing such a temperature is good for is to expand metals and make beer merchants happy.' According to Bernard, who was probably romancing, Cézanne called out 'Pontier! Pontier!' on his deathbed. Auguste-Henri Pontier (Director of Musée Granet) refused to allow any Cézanne canvasses to enter the Aix museum during his lifetime. Pontier died in 1926 by which time the town could no longer afford them. 'All my compatriots are arseholes compared to me. I should have told you I received the cocoa.' (Cézanne's final letter to his son, 15th October 1906.)

> The grapes are caught
> in the act of disappearing,
> moving, as Rilke said
> the angels moved, between
> the living and the dead.

I have written the date, Penultimate day and Cloudy in my notebook. The valley seems swabbed and swaddled, the occasional plane-groan or bee-sound picked out for peculiar emphasis. And yes, the chief beauty is light, breaking the world into highlights and lowlights, mid-tones, far-flung affinities. In the very late watercolours, agitated brushwork, writhing blurs of aqueous blue and sharp yellow, riparian activities (wrestling, swimming, stooping, striding, reclining, combing, drying, squatting) dissolve into light, into curvilinear outlines, vertical striations, scattered blotches.

A late butterfly
  contends with
the first autumn wind.

Its jittery nowhere-
  for-certain
flight seems erratic

but might not be.

I have retrieved the wheelie bag from under the bed and left it under a pine tree next to the track. Someone will pick it up. Walking back to the hut one last time, time has been deleted. I might have arrived yesterday, giving Gary a final hug. I might have walked back from the cliffs, chilly from missing a sunset, my father's pockets full of balled-up copper wire. I sit to the same view through the same drystone arch. Now the light has withdrawn, the dust-path in the foreground is barely dappled, the precise pink-grey almost impossible to catch. The limestone ridge, bathed in half-shadow, absorbs everything, even the bleach-blue sky, cloudless now with the barest edge of cold. So, I'm pursuing my researches, if a little laboriously. And Cézanne is right of course; we experience nature more in depth than in surface. Looking up from my book, I can see he has added vibrations of light in red and yellow, then a sufficient quantity of blue tones to give the feel of air.

Acknowledgements

I am very grateful to Alex Danchev, whose biography, *Cézanne: A Life* (Profile Books, 2013) as well as his wonderful translation of *The Letters of Paul Cézanne* (Thames and Hudson, 2013) were oreintating concerns of this haibun. Alex died suddenly and tragically not long after I interviewed him for *PoetryEast*. Christopher Lloyds's beautiful and insightful book, *Paul Cézanne's Drawings and Watercolours* (Thames and Hudson, 2015) was also an important inspiration. *A Cézanne Haibun* was originally intended to form part of my forthcoming collection, *After Cézanne* (Bloodaxe Books, 2019) but it would have made the collection too long.

My thanks go to Ann and Peter Sansom for agreeing to publish *A Cézanne Haibun* and for their help and encouragement; to Bernard O'Donoghue for reading it in manuscript; and to Warren Davis for his proof-reading and editorial suggestions. I am especially grateful to Mimi Khalvati, without whose help and guidance this haibun could not have been written. And I am greatly indebted to the to the Arts Council England for their generous support.

Maitreyabandhu's first pamphlet *The Bond* won the Poetry Business Book and Pamphlet Competition and was shortlisted for the Michael Marks Award. His debut collection, *The Crumb Road* (Bloodaxe, 2013) is a PBS Recommendation. *Yarn* (also with Bloodaxe) was published in autumn 2015. Maitreyabandhu lives and works at the London Buddhist Centre and has been ordained into the Triratna Buddhist Order for 28 years. He has written three books on Buddhism.